WITCHES DANCE

(Le Streghe)

for Violin and Piano

T0195272

NICCOLÒ PAGANINI, Op. 8

Violino.

INTRODUZIONE.

PIANO.

Maestoso.

f *p* *f* *p*

6

f *sul ponticello* *pp*

f *pp*

9

cresc.

cresc.

Copyright © 2015 The Jascha Heifetz Estate
Sole selling agent Lauren Keiser Music Publishing (ASCAP).
International Copyright Secured. All rights reserved.

Digital and photographic copying of this page is illegal.

Digital and photographic copying of this page is illegal.

Digital and photographic copying of this page is illegal.

Digital and photographic copying of this page is illegal.

Digital and photographic copying of this page is illegal.

Digital and photographic copying of this page is illegal.

Digital and photographic copying of this page is illegal.

Digital and photographic copying of this page is illegal.

Digital and photographic copying of this page is illegal.

Digital and photographic copying of this page is illegal.

Digital and photographic copying of this page is illegal.

EDITOR'S NOTE

Niccolò Paganini's (1782-1840) *Witches' Dance* begins with a quasi-operatic Introduction followed by a Theme and Variations. (Theme by Franz Xaver Süssmayr).

A mature work of Paganini, it uses all the innovations the composer introduced: double stops, three and four part chords in rapid successions, harmonics in single and double notes, left hand pizzicato, scales and arpeggios using the entire range of the instrument. This work, like so many others by Paganini has not been published during the composer's lifetime.

This Critical Urtext edition is based on the very first edition of the work. Jascha Heifetz' bowings, fingerings and his suggestions regarding interpretation are integral part of this edition.

Endre Granat